READING POWER

The Inventions of

Alexander Graham Bell

The Telephone

Holly Cefrey

The Rosen Publishing Group's
PowerKids Press™
New York

Published in 2003 by The Rosen Publishing Group, Inc.
29 East 21st Street, New York, NY 10010

First Edition

Book Design: Daniel Hosek

Photo Credits: Cover, pp. 8, 9, 13 (foreground), 14, 14–15, 20 © Culver Pictures; pp. 5, 6 Library of Congress, Prints and Photographs Division; pp. 7, 11, 13 (background) Library of Congress, Manuscript Division; pp. 17, 18, 19, 21 Parks Canada/Alexander Graham Bell National Historic Site of Canada

Library of Congress Cataloging-in-Publication Data

Cefrey, Holly.
The inventions of Alexander Graham Bell : the telephone / Holly
Cefrey.
    p. cm. — (19th century American inventors)
Summary: A brief biography of Alexander Graham Bell, focusing on his invention of the telephone and his lifelong work with deaf people.
Includes bibliographical references and index.
ISBN 0-8239-6441-8 (library binding)
1. Bell, Alexander Graham, 1847-1922—Juvenile literature. 2. Inventors—United States—Biography—Juvenile literature. [1. Bell, Alexander Graham, 1847-1922. 2. Inventors.] I. Title. II. Series.
TK6143.B4 C43 2003
621.385'092—dc21

                                    2002000096

]

Contents

Young Bell

Alexander Graham Bell was born in Edinburgh, Scotland, on March 3, 1847, to Alexander and Eliza Bell. Even though Mrs. Bell was deaf, she was young Bell's main teacher.

Alexander Bell was the second of three sons. He was close to his family.

The Fact Box

At age 11, Bell added Graham as his middle name. Graham was a close family friend and Bell respected him. Young Bell was called Graham by his family and friends.

Bell's father taught people who were deaf how to speak. He invented a method called Visible Speech. He taught young Bell how to use Visible Speech.

Bell and his father

Young Bell was interested in speech and how sounds were made. He and his brothers helped their father show others how to use Visible Speech.

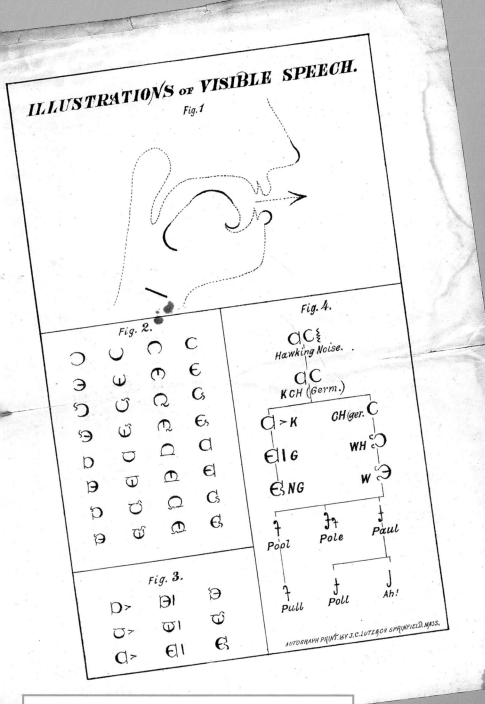

Visible Speech uses written symbols that show the positions of the throat, the tongue, and the lips when speaking.

7

Teacher and Inventor

In 1871, Bell and his family moved to the United States. He lived in Boston, Massachusetts, and began teaching at a school for the Deaf. During this time, Bell became interested in making the telegraph better. Bell's idea was to send people's voices over telegraph wires.

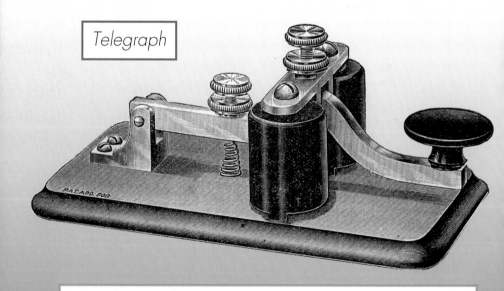

Telegraph

Telegraphs use electricity to send clicks over wires. These clicks spell out words.

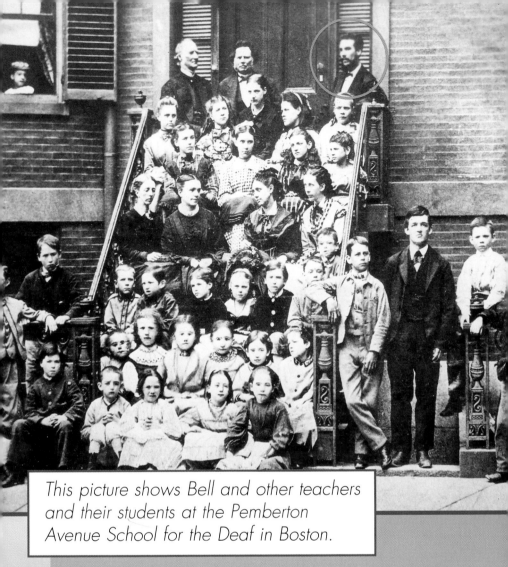

This picture shows Bell and other teachers and their students at the Pemberton Avenue School for the Deaf in Boston.

The Fact Box

Bell became an American citizen in 1882.

The Telephone

Bell did not have the skill needed to make the parts for his invention. He hired Thomas A. Watson to help him build a machine that could send voices over wires. Bell was given money for his work by the fathers of two of his students.

Thomas Watson was born on January 18, 1854, in Salem, Massachusetts. After working with Bell, he went on to run his own shipbuilding business. He also acted in plays.

11

Bell's invention, the telephone, first worked on March 10, 1876. The two parts of his invention were connected by wires. One part sent sound, and the other part received the sound. Bell put each part in a different room. When Bell spoke into one part, Watson could hear and understand him through the other part.

"I then shouted . . . the following sentence: 'Mr. Watson—come here—I want to see you.' To my delight, he came and declared that he heard and understood what I said."
—from Alexander Graham Bell's notebook

Before he built his telephone, Bell drew pictures of his idea for it in his notebook.

An early model of Bell's telephone from 1875

Bell wanted to show his invention to as many people as he could. In 1876, Bell showed his invention at the Centennial Exhibition in Philadelphia, Pennsylvania. People were amazed to see what Bell had invented.

The Centennial Exhibition was a celebration of the one hundredth birthday of the United States.

Bell's first telephone did not work as well as today's telephones. Sometimes, he had to shout for his voice to be heard at the other end.

After the Telephone

In July 1877, Bell formed the Bell Telephone Company to provide telephone service in the United States. In 1880, Bell won a science prize from France for his work. It was called the Volta Prize. He used the prize money of $10,000 to set up a lab. One of his first new inventions was a machine that helped people who had breathing problems.

In 1893, Bell used money he earned from his new inventions to build the Volta Bureau. The Bureau carries on Bell's work for the Deaf. It is located in Washington, D.C.

Bell also made a kite that was so strong, it could lift a person off the ground. Then, he made a fast boat that moved over the water. It used metal plates that looked like skis. It was called a hydrofoil.

Hydrofoil

Bell's kite

Fun Facts

- In 1878, Rutherford B. Hayes was the first U.S. president to have a telephone in the White House. The first call he made was to Alexander Graham Bell.

- Bell was interested in airplanes. He helped invent a movable part of an airplane wing that controls the way the plane flies.

- Bell and his staff invented airplane landing gear that allowed planes to take off and land on fields.

Lasting Inventions

Bell continued to think of new ideas until he died on August 2, 1922. His inventions and ideas will never be forgotten because so many of them are still in use. Some of Alexander Graham Bell's ideas are still becoming new inventions today.

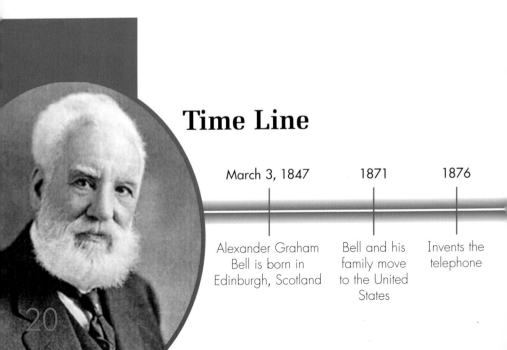

Time Line

March 3, 1847	1871	1876
Alexander Graham Bell is born in Edinburgh, Scotland	Bell and his family move to the United States	Invents the telephone

As an inventor, Bell invented many things to make life easier.

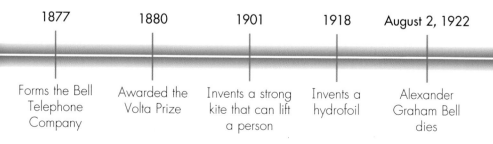

1877	1880	1901	1918	August 2, 1922
Forms the Bell Telephone Company	Awarded the Volta Prize	Invents a strong kite that can lift a person	Invents a hydrofoil	Alexander Graham Bell dies

Glossary

celebration (sehl-uh-**bray**-shuhn) special services in honor of a person, act, time, or day

Centennial Exhibition (sehn-**tehn**-ee-uhl ehk-suh-**bihsh**-uhn) a fair celebrating the one hundredth birthday of the United States (1776–1876)

deaf (**dehf**) not able to hear

hydrofoil (**hy**-druh-foil) a fast boat that uses ski-like metal plates to move over the water

invention (ihn-**vehn**-shuhn) something new that someone thinks of or creates

lab (**lab**) a room or building with special equipment where scientists do tests and experiments

landing gear (**lan**-dihng **gihr**) a special part of an airplane that lets planes take off and land

main (**mayn**) most important

symbol (**sihm**-buhl) something that stands for something else

telegraph (**tehl**-uh-graf) a machine that sends coded messages over wires using electricity

Visible Speech (**vihz**-uh-buhl **speech**) a set of symbols that shows the human mouth forming sounds, used to help the Deaf to speak

Resources

Books

Alexander Graham Bell
by Leonard Everett Fisher
Atheneum (1999)

Alexander Graham Bell
by Struan Reid
Heinemann Library (2000)

Web Sites

Due to the changing nature of Internet links, PowerKids Press has developed an on-line list of Web sites related to the subjects of this book. This site is updated regularly. Please use this link to access the list:

http://www.powerkidslinks.com/ncai/iagb/

Index

Word Count: 491

Note to Librarians, Teachers, and Parents

If reading is a challenge, Reading Power is a solution! Reading Power is perfect for readers who want high-interest subject matter at an accessible reading level. These fact-filled, photo-illustrated books are designed for readers who want straightforward vocabulary, engaging topics, and a manageable reading experience. With clear picture/text correspondence, leveled Reading Power books put the reader in charge. Now readers have the power to get the information they want and the skills they need in a user-friendly format.